States

ALABAMA

by Jason Kirchner

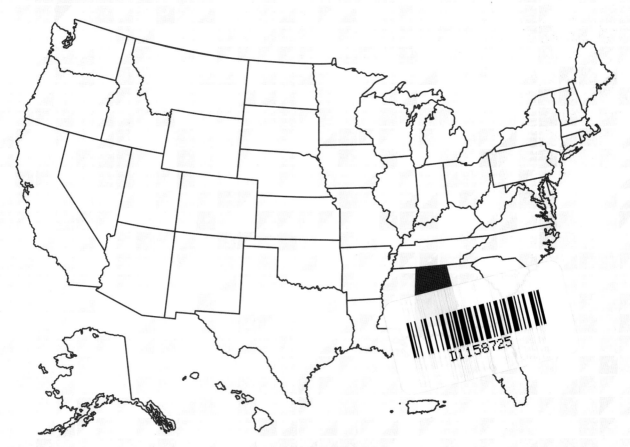

D1158725

CAPSTONE PRESS
a capstone imprint

Next Page Books are published by Capstone Press,
1710 Roe Crest Drive, North Mankato, Minnesota 56003
www.mycapstone.com

Library of Congress Cataloging-in-Publication Data
Cataloging-in-publication information is on file with the Library of
Congress.
ISBN 978-1-5157-0386-0 (library binding)
ISBN 978-1-5157-0447-8 (paperback)
ISBN 978-1-5157-0499-7 (ebook PDF)

Editorial Credits
Jaclyn Jaycox, editor; Ashlee Suker, designer; Morgan Walters,
media researcher; Laura Manthe, production specialist

Photo Credits
Alamy: North Wind Picture Archive, 12, Walker Art Library, 25;
Capstone Library: bottom right 20; Capstone Press: Angi Gahler, (flag,
seal) 22-23; Corbis: Tarker, 13; CriaImages.com: Jay Robert Nash
Collection, middle 19; Library of Congress: O. Fernandez, 28, Harris
& Ewing, bottom 18, George F. Landegger Collection of Alabama
Photographs in Carol M. Highsmith's America, 10, Warren K. Leffler,
top 19; Newscom: Everett Collection, top 18; One Mile Up, Inc: map
4,7; Shutterstock: 360b, middle 18, 29, Alf Ribeiro, 14, Bildagentur
Zoonar GmbH, bottom 24, Charles Knowles, 6, Goran Bogicevic, top
24, HodagMedia, 17, Jason Patrick Ross, bottom right 21, Jeffrey B.
Banke, top left 21, Jeffrey M. Frank, 7, Leong9655, 27, Maria Komar,
top right 20, Philip Arno Photography, 16, Rob Hainer, 5, right 8, 11,
s_bukley, bottom 19, schankz, bottom left 21, Shackleford-Photography,
Cover, left 8, tab62, top right 21, Teresa Levite, middle right 21, Vitaly
Ilyasov, bottom left 20, Yermolov, 15; U.S. Geological Survey: middle left
21; Wikimedia: Bill Varnedoe, 9, The New York Public Library, Digital
Gallery, 26, USDA Forest ServiceSRS-4552/Erich G. Vallery, top left 20

All Design Elements by Shutterstock

Printed and bound in China.
0316/CA21600187
012016   009436F16

TABLE OF CONTENTS

Want to take your research further? Ask your librarian if your school subscribes to PebbleGo Next. If so, when you see this helpful symbol (↖) throughout the book, log onto www.pebblegonext.com for bonus downloads and information.

LOCATION

Alabama is one of the nation's southern states. Mississippi lies to its west, and Georgia is on its east. To the north is Tennessee. Florida and the Gulf of Mexico are south of Alabama. Only a small piece of southwestern Alabama reaches the Gulf of Mexico. Montgomery is Alabama's capital. Alabama's biggest cities are Montgomery, Birmingham, Mobile, and Huntsville.

PebbleGo Next Bonus!
To print and label your own map, search keywords:
AL MAP

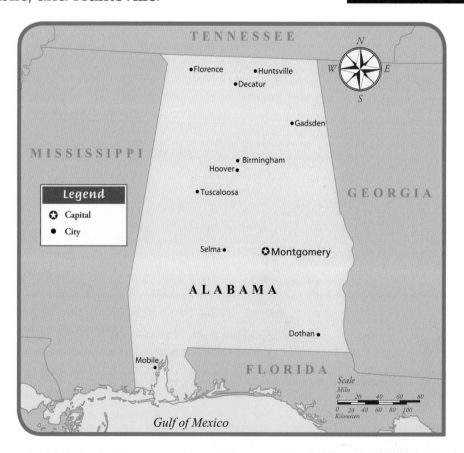

Alabama's state capitol building is located in the city of Montgomery.

GEOGRAPHY

Alabama is home to many landscapes. The Gulf Coastal Plain covers two-thirds of Alabama. Pine forests cover the northern part of the plain. The flat, southwestern part is covered with wetlands. The Piedmont Plateau is in east-central Alabama. Cheaha Mountain, the highest point in the state, is in this area. Cheaha Mountain is 2,407 feet (734 meters) high. Farther northwest is the Appalachian Plateau. This land is lower and flatter. The Valley and Ridge region is a set of long, narrow valleys between mountain ridges. The Interior Low Plateaus are rolling lands in the northwestern part of the state.

An overlook offers Cheaha State Park visitors a view of the Piedmont Plateau.

Legend

▲ Highest Point

○ Point of Interest

⌇ River

Tennessee River

INTERIOR LOW PLATEAUS

DeSoto Caverns

APPALACHIAN PLATEAU

VALLEY AND RIDGE

▲ Cheaha Mountain

GULF COASTAL PLAIN

PIEDMONT PLATEAU

Tombigbee River

Alabama River

Chattahoochee River

Mobile River

Scale
Miles
0   20   40   60   80

0   20   40   60   80   100
Kilometers

Mobile Bay

Gulf of Mexico

N
W   E
S

WEATHER

Alabama has mild weather. The average winter temperature in Alabama is 47 degrees Fahrenheit (8 degrees Celsius). The average summer temperature is 79°F (26°C).

Average High and Low Temperatures (Montgomery, AL)

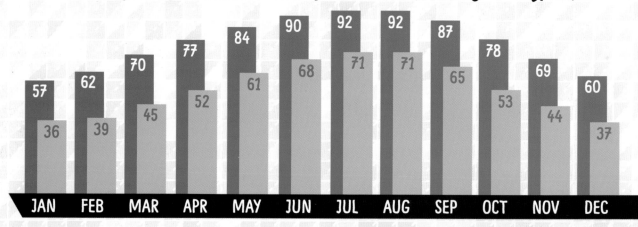

	JAN	FEB	MAR	APR	MAY	JUN	JUL	AUG	SEP	OCT	NOV	DEC
High	57	62	70	77	84	90	92	92	87	78	69	60
Low	36	39	45	52	61	68	71	71	65	53	44	37

DeSoto Caverns

DeSoto Caverns is found in Childersburg, in the foothills of the Appalachian Mountains in north-central Alabama. Visitors view thousands of cave formations that are 12 stories underground.

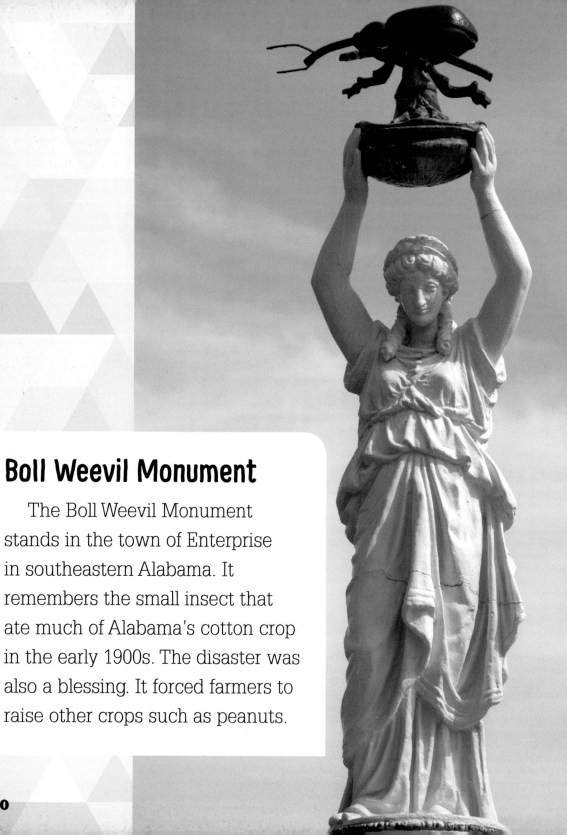

Boll Weevil Monument

The Boll Weevil Monument stands in the town of Enterprise in southeastern Alabama. It remembers the small insect that ate much of Alabama's cotton crop in the early 1900s. The disaster was also a blessing. It forced farmers to raise other crops such as peanuts.

Little River Canyon

The Little River Canyon in northeastern Alabama is one of the state's natural wonders. Most of Little River flows atop Lookout Mountain. It flows into the canyon, creating a 45-foot (14-meter) waterfall. The area also has boulders, bluffs, and sandstone cliffs. Visitors hike, fish, and camp in the area.

HISTORY AND GOVERNMENT

An early Native American village in Alabama as described by Hernando De Soto in 1540.

People were living in Alabama thousands of years ago. Cliff dwellers lived in northern Alabama. Mound builders lived near Tuscaloosa. Later many American Indian groups settled in Alabama. Spanish explorer Alonso Álvarez de Piñeda sailed into Mobile Bay in southwestern Alabama in 1519. Hernando de Soto explored Alabama in 1540. In 1702 the French founded Fort Louis near the Mobile River. The fort was moved to present-day Mobile in 1711.

In 1783 the American colonies won independence from Great Britain in the Revolutionary War (1775–1783). Much of Alabama became part of the United States. In 1817 Alabama became a U.S. territory. Alabama became the 22nd state in 1819.

Hernando de Soto arrived in Florida and took his expedition through the southeast states, including Alabama.

Alabama's state government has three branches. The governor leads the executive branch, which carries out laws. The legislature is made up of the 35-member Senate and the 105-member House of Representatives. Judges and their courts make up the judicial branch. They uphold the laws.

INDUSTRY

Cotton was once the center of Alabama's economy, but insects called boll weevils destroyed cotton crops in 1913. It forced farmers to raise other crops. Today cotton is still one of Alabama's top crops. Farmers also grow corn, soybeans, peanuts, wheat, and other crops. Young chickens called broilers bring in more than 50 percent of Alabama's farm income.

A cotton picker harvests the field by automatically separating the cotton from the plant.

Manufacturing is a leading industry in Alabama. Factories in the state make transportation equipment, chemicals, and paper products. Steelmaking is another important industry. Many steel mills operate in Birmingham in north-central Alabama.

Mining is a small but important part of Alabama's economy. Most of the state's coal is found in northern Alabama. Oil and natural gas are drilled in the southern part of the state.

Service industries are the largest industry in Alabama today. Most Alabamians work in service industries, such as trade, finance, and insurance.

A ladle pours hot steel into a mold as part of the steelmaking process.

POPULATION

Alabama has a larger African-American population than most states. About one of every four people in Alabama is African-American. Most live in large cities and in southern Alabama. More than 3 million white people live in Alabama. Most of the state's white people are descendants of early settlers. They may have roots in Ireland, England, or Germany. A small number of Alabamians are Hispanic, Asian, or American Indian.

Population by Ethnicity

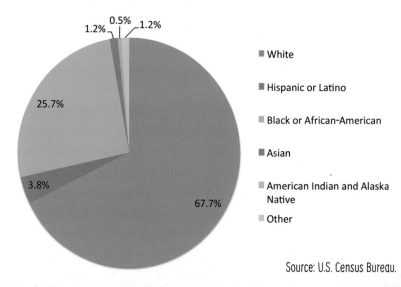

1.2% 0.5% 1.2%

25.7%

3.8%

67.7%

- White
- Hispanic or Latino
- Black or African-American
- Asian
- American Indian and Alaska Native
- Other

Source: U.S. Census Bureau.

Thousands of people attend the Grand Prix of Alabama each year in Birmingham.

FAMOUS PEOPLE

Rosa Parks (1913-2005) was a civil rights activist. In 1955 she was arrested for refusing to give up her bus seat to a white passenger. Many consider this to be the beginning of the civil rights movement. She was born in Tuskegee.

Condoleezza Rice (1954–) became the first woman to serve as U.S. national security adviser. President George W. Bush appointed her in 2001. She then served as the United States secretary of state from 2005 to 2009. She was born in Birmingham.

Helen Keller (1880–1968) was an author and educator who worked for the rights of people with handicaps. She lost her sight and hearing before she was 2 years old. She was born in Tuscumbia.

Coretta Scott King (1927–2006) was a civil rights leader. Her husband was Dr. Martin Luther King Jr. After he was shot and killed in 1968, she continued his work. She was born in Marion.

Nat "King" Cole (1919–1965) was a popular singer, pianist, and actor. He was called "the man with the velvet voice." "Mona Lisa" and "Unforgettable" were two of his hit songs. He was born in Montgomery.

Courteney Cox (1964–) is an award-winning actress. She has appeared in many movies and TV shows, including the TV show *Friends*. She was born in Birmingham.

STATE SYMBOLS

Tree

southern longleaf pine

Flower

camellia

Bird

yellowhammer

Horse

racking horse

PebbleGo Next Bonus! To make a popular Alabama dessert, search keywords:
AL RECIPE

Game bird

wild turkey

Nut

pecan

Amphibian

Red Hills salamander

Wildflower

oak-leaf hydrangea

Rock

marble

Insect

monarch butterfly

FAST FACTS

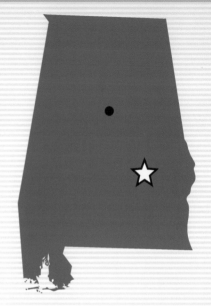

STATEHOOD
1819

CAPITAL ☆
Montgomery

LARGEST CITY •
Birmingham

SIZE
50,645 square miles (131,171 square kilometers)
land area (2010 U.S. Census Bureau)

POPULATION
4,833,722 (2013 U.S. Census estimate)

STATE NICKNAME
Heart of Dixie, Cotton State

STATE MOTTO
"Audemus jura nostra defendere," which is Latin
for "We dare defend our rights."

STATE SEAL

Alabama's state seal features a map of Alabama showing its major rivers and bordering states. Alabama's rivers were important shipping routes in the state's early days. Today they are a source of hydroelectric power, a form of energy produced by flowing water.

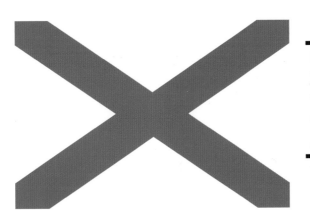

PebbleGo Next Bonus!
To print and color
your own flag,
search keywords:

AL FLAG

STATE FLAG

The Alabama state flag was adopted in 1895. It shows an X-shaped red cross on a white background. This symbol appeared on Confederate flags during the Civil War. The X-shaped cross is also called a Saint Andrew's cross. Saint Andrew was an early Christian saint.

MINING PRODUCTS

coal, natural gas, petroleum, portland cement, limestone

MANUFACTURED GOODS

motor vehicle parts, petroleum and coal products, chemicals, paper, food products, fabricated metal products, transportation equipment, plastics and rubber products, computer and electronic equipment

FARM PRODUCTS

chickens, hogs, beef cattle, eggs, peanuts, soybeans, cotton

PebbleGo Next Bonus!
To learn the lyrics to the state song, search keywords:
AL SONG

ALABAMA TIMELINE

1519 Spanish explorer Alonso Álvarez de Piñeda sails into Mobile Bay.

1540 Spanish explorer Hernando de Soto explores much of present-day Alabama.

1620 The Pilgrims establish a colony in the New World in present-day Massachusetts.

1702 French settlers set up Fort Louis near the Mobile River.

1783

The American colonies win independence from Great Britain in the Revolutionary War (1775–1783). The United States gains much of Alabama from Great Britain.

1814

The Battle of Horseshoe Bend in central Alabama led by General Andrew Jackson ends in defeat for the Creek Indians. The Indians are forced to give up their land.

1817

Alabama Territory is created.

1819

Alabama becomes the 22nd state on December 14.

1861

Alabama leaves the United States to join a new country called the Confederate States of America. Montgomery becomes the first capital of the Confederacy.

1861–1865

World War II is fought; the United States enters the war in 1941.

1868

The Union and the Confederacy fight the Civil War. Alabama fights for the Confederacy. About 122,000 Alabamians fight in the war, and 45,000 Alabamians die in it.

1913

A small insect called the boll weevil destroys most of Alabama's cotton crop.

1914–1918

World War I is fought; the United States enters the war in 1917.

1939-1945 World War II is fought; the United States enters the war in 1941.

1955 African-American Rosa Parks is arrested for not giving up her bus seat to a white passenger. Montgomery's bus boycott begins.

1965 Civil rights leader Dr. Martin Luther King Jr. leads protesters on a march from Selma to Montgomery. It leads to the Voting Rights Act of 1965.

PebbleGo Next Bonus!
To watch a video about
the National Voting Rights
Museum, search keywords:
AL VIDEO

1985 The Tennessee-Tombigbee Waterway opens. Located in Mississippi and Alabama, it serves as an important transportation route to the Gulf of Mexico. It is the largest water resource project ever built in the United States.

2001 On September 11 terrorists attack the World Trade Center and the Pentagon.

2001 Alabama native Condoleezza Rice becomes the first woman to be appointed national security adviser.

2006 Judge Sue Bell Cobb becomes the first woman to be elected chief justice of the Alabama Supreme Court.

2010 An explosion on an offshore oil rig kills 11 people and causes millions of gallons of oil to pour into the Gulf of Mexico. Oil from the spill reaches Alabama's coast, harming fish and the state's tourism industry.

2015 University of West Alabama participates in first ever World Antibiotic Awareness Week in November.

Glossary

bluff *(BLUFF)*—a tall, steep bank or cliff

descendant *(di-SEN-duhnt)*—your descendants are your children, their children, and so on into the future.

disaster *(di-ZAS-tuhr)*—an event that causes great damage, loss, or suffering

economy *(i-KAH-nuh-mee)*—the ways in which a state handles its money and resources

executive *(ig-ZE-kyuh-tiv)*—the branch of government that makes sure laws are followed

formation *(for-MAY-shuhn)*—a pattern or a shape

industry *(IN-duh-stree)*—a business which produces a product or provides a service

legislature *(LEJ-iss-lay-chur)*—a group of elected officials who have the power to make or change laws for a country or state

petroleum *(puh-TROH-lee-uhm)*—an oily liquid found below the earth's surface used to make gasoline, heating oil, and many other products

plateau *(pla-TOH)*—an area of high, flat land

region *(REE-juhn)*—a large area

Read More

Ganeri, Anita. *United States of America: A Benjamin Blog and His Inquisitive Dog Guide.* Country Guides. Chicago: Heinemann Raintree, 2015.

Hart, Joyce. *Alabama.* It's My State! New York: Cavendish Square Pub., 2016.

Kallio, Jamie. *What's Great About Alabama?* Our Great States. Minneapolis: Lerner Publications, 2015.

Internet Sites

FactHound offers a safe, fun way to find Internet sites related to this book. All of the sites on FactHound have been researched by our staff.

Here's all you do:

Visit www.facthound.com

Type in this code: 9781515703860

Check out projects, games and lots more at
www.capstonekids.com

Critical Thinking Using the Common Core

1. The Boll Weevil Monument in the town of Enterprise remembers the small insect that ate much of Alabama's cotton crop in the early 1900s. The disaster was also a blessing because it forced farmers to raise other crops. What kinds of crops are important to Alabama's economy now? (Key Ideas and Details)

2. In 1955 Rosa Parks was arrested for refusing to give up her bus seat to a white passenger. Many people consider this the beginning of the civil rights movement. Why was this event important? (Integration of Knowledge and Ideas)

3. Look at the landmarks on pages 9-11. Which one would you most like to visit? Why? (Integration of Knowledge and Ideas)

Index